QUO VADIS?

The Subversion of the Catholic Church

Piers Paul Read

The Claridge Press
London

First published in Great Britain 1991

by The Claridge Press
6 Linden Gardens
London W2 4ES

Copyright   ©   Piers Paul Read

Printed by
Short Run Press
Exeter, Devon

ISBN 1-870626-08-7

Read, Piers Paul: *Quo Vadis?: The Subversion of the Catholic Church*

1. Religion

QUO VADIS?

Catholics should be fully aware of the real freedom to speak their minds which stems from 'a feeling for the faith' and from love. It stems from that feeling for the faith which is aroused and nourished by the spirit of truth in order that, under the guidance of the teaching of the Church which they accept with reverence, the People of God may cling unswervingly to the faith given to the early Church, with true judgement penetrate its meaning more deeply, and apply it more fully in their lives.

Vatican II, Pastoral Instruction on the Means of Social
Communication (*Communio et Progressio*)

The Decade of Evangelisation

What do Catholics believe? The call for a decade of evangelisation comes at a time when there is as much confusion about doctrine as at any time since the Reformation. What Alain Besançon says of France is equally true of England: 'Within the Catholic world today, there is a divergence among some authors that is far wider than the gap which separated Calvin from the Council of Trent but the church adopts no position. It does not say what is true and what is false.'[1] The Pope says one thing and the theologians another, while the Catholic bishops of England and Wales act like umpires whose only purpose is to see fair play.

Compare three recently published opinions by Catholics on the critical question of whether or not it is necessary to believe in Christ. 'There is salvation in no one else,' writes the Pope, quoting St. Paul, in his appeal for a new missionary age, 'for there is no other name under heaven given among men by which we must be saved'[2].

But 'Since the Church has expressed repentance (however muted) for its previous attitude towards other religions,' asks Donald Nicol, once rector of the Ecumenical Institute at Tantur, 'and now acknowledges the "seeds of the Spirit" in other religions and grants that adherents of these religions may come to salvation by way of their religions, does it not follow that there is now no need for evangelization?' Can the Church still insist upon 'the uniqueness of Christ'?[3]

Certainly, rejoins the Pope. 'One of the most serious reasons for the lack of interest in the missionary task is a widespread indifferentism which, sad to say, is found also among Christians. It is based on incorrect theological perspectives and is characterised by a religious relativism which leads to the belief that "one religion is as good as another"'.[4]

And what do we hear from an English bishop? 'The Decade of Evangelisation poses no threat to anyone,' writes the Right Rev Gerald Mahon, the auxilliary bishop of West London. 'It is directed first of all to spreading the gospel among people who think they are Christians.'[5]

There is confusion not just about what the Church teaches but also about what the Church is; for it has been put about, and is now commonly believed, that the Second Vatican Council abandoned the Catholic claim to an unique authority as the Church founded by Christ; that it pronounced the Catholic Church to be but a branch of the Christian Church, and Christianity, like Judaism and Islam, part of a universal montheistic religion.

It is precisely arguments of this kind which are condemned by Pope John Paul II in his encyclical letter, *Redemptoris Missio.* 'The most insidious of these excuses [for not evangelizing] are certainly the ones which people claim to find support for in such and such a teaching of the Council'[6]; yet they are implicit, as we shall see, in the religious instruction given to Catholic children in Catholic schools. Because few Catholics have actually read the decrees of Vatican II, 'progressive' theologians and 'renewing' catechists are able to postulate a revolution in Catholic thinking which in fact never took place. For the sake of Christian unity, they suggest, the Council subjected the Pope to the bishops and included other Christian denominations into the 'one true church'. As a result the Eucharist is no longer a sacrifice, nor is the bread and wine in any literal sense the body and blood of Christ. Personal confession has been replaced by a communal 'reconciliation', and sin is now a relative term because the Council declared the sovereignty of conscience. The sacramental Church, the hierarchical Church, the Church which subordinates 'the visible to the invisible, action to contemplation, and this present world to that city yet to come'[7] was wound up by Vatican II.

In their zeal to rid the church of redundant superstitions, these iconoclasts either ignore or deny whole areas of the Church's teaching, and in doing so they destroy the *coherence* of Christian belief. As Nietzsche realised, 'Christianity is a system, a consistently thought out and *complete* view of things. If one breaks out of it a fundamental idea...one thereby breaks the whole thing to pieces'.[8] It is impossible to reject or ignore the the idea of Hell, for example, or Original Sin, without subverting the very idea of Revelation.

It must be acknowledged, of course, that in a society which is overwhelmingly agnostic, and a nation that is determinedly matter-of-fact, it is not easy to insist upon the audacious hypotheses which make up the Christian religion. A further disadvantage is a prevalent ignorance of history in the younger generation to whom the antiquity of the Catholic Church means nothing at all. It may trace its ancestry back two thousand years to the reign of Octavius Caesar, and join together the two ages of human civilisation, as Lord Macaulay wrote, and in the Pope boast a pedigree 'beside which the proudest royal houses are but of yesterday'. To the young in the market for a religion, however, the Catholic Church is on the same supermarket shelf as the Anglican, Muslim, Buddhist, Baptist and Pentecostalist religions. Indeed, one of the very reasons why so much is made of Vatican II is the assumption among many that what is old must somehow be wrong: 'mediaeval' or 'primitive' are terms of intellectual abuse used by those who have never read Aquinas, Boethius or Plato.

Moreover, in a society where the only truth is one arrived at by science or agreed by public opinion, the idea of Revelation is difficult to convey. But Revelation is integral to the Christian religion — the proposition that God has spoken to man through the prophets of Israel and then 'Jesus Christ, the eternal pastor, [who] set up the holy Church by entrusting the apostles with their mission as he himself had been sent by the Father...'[9] The idea of authority, too, is distasteful in a society which believes that everyone is entitled to his own opinion.

Of course over the ages there have been disputes, often bitter, between different theological schools about unsettled points of doctrine, and from time to time there have arisen distinct factions — Pelagians, Paulicians, Nestorians, Calvinists, Lutherans, Jansenists, Quietists, Modernists — some of which survive as distinct Christian churches; but always within the Catholic Church there has prevailed a concept of orthodoxy about the core of its beliefs constantly taught by the *magisterium* — viz the bishops throughout the world in communion with the successor of St Peter — which would be readily acknowledged by St. Paul in the first century, St. Augustine in the fourth, St. Thomas Aquinas in the fourteenth, St. Thomas More in the sixteenth, St. Francis of Sales in the seventeenth, Cardinal Newman in the nineteenth, or Cardinal Ratzinger today: but would any of them recognize it in *Weaving the Web*, a course of religious instruction that is being used in Catholic schools in England today?

Vatican II

Since the decrees of the Second Vatican Council are so often used to justify the 'new look' in Catholic thinking, it is necessary to consider why it was called and what it said.

When Pope John XXIII summoned the Council, it was not to decide upon questions about the faith of the Catholic Church, but to consider how Catholics should live according to that faith in the post-war world. Since the Middle Ages, when the concept of Christendom had matched, more or less, the frontiers of Europe and most of Europe had recognised the spiritual primacy of the Pope, the Church had regarded such a theocratic society as the norm, and had reacted to deviations such as the Reformation in Germany or the Revolution in France with enduring hostility.

Certainly, this hostility was partly justified by the fact that these movements were largely directed against the Church; but the attitude of the Church often amounted to closing a door after the horse had bolted, and certain ideas which had become commonplace as time went on — democracy, say, or the rights of man — continued to be regarded with suspicion by the Church.

There were many notable attempts by different Popes to adjust to the changing world — by Leo XIII, for example — but there was a sense in which the Catholic Church at the time of World War II was still an ideological fortress — magnificent, perhaps, but enclosed by its ramparts and so limited in its influence. The salt had not lost its taste, but too much of it remained in the tin.

Moreover the defensive attitude towards all that was not Catholic had led both to a cut-and-dried interpretation of its teaching, encapsulated in the Penny Catechism, and a belligerent exaggeration of the importance of certain inessential differences with the Catholic Church and other Christian denominations such as saying the mass in Latin or abstaining from meat on Fridays.

Thus the Council called by John XXIII was not a *dogmatic* council but a *pastoral* one — a gathering of bishops from all over the world to consider how their flocks should be directed to approach the world outside the Church. It was not, in this respect, called to hold a *post mortem* over mistakes made in the past, but rather to look into the future by reading 'the signs of the times'.

John XXIII must have felt, with some justification, that these signs should not be read by the Pope alone. It was unstated, but there inevitably hovered over Vatican II, as it hovers over the postwar consciousness of half the world, the extermination of the Jews in the concentrations camps of Nazi Germany. It was not, as is commonly believed, that the Church had remained indifferent to this nadir in the moral development of man: as a former Israeli consul in Italy acknowledged, 'the Catholic Church saved more Jewish lives during the war than all the other Churches, religious institutions and rescue organisations put together...'[10]

No one knew this better than Pope John XXIII who as Apostolic Delegate in Ankara during the war had himself organised the rescue of many Jews. However it was indisputable that the virulent anti-semitism which found expression in the Holocaust had sprung from the heartland of Catholic Europe — from Austria, for example, or Croatia.

Here again, it is erroneous to suggest that because Hitler and Himmler came from Catholic countries, their crimes can be blamed on the Catholic Church which, after the destruction of the Communist and Socialist parties in Germany and Austria, remained the only social force to oppose the Nazis. But what must have been apparent

to the Pope was that his predecessors, Pius XI and XII, had misread
the signs of the times in seeing Bolshevism as a greater threat than
fascism to both the Church and the world.

Again, the mistake is not difficult to understand. Pius XI had
witnessed the fierce persecution of the Orthodox Church after the
Revolution in Russia, and Pius XII, as Nuncio in Munich in 1919, had
been threatened at gunpoint by the Spartacist revolutionaries. He
suffered from nightmares about it for the rest of his life. Add to this
the experience of the first months of the Spanish Civil War in which
12 bishops, 283 nuns, 2365 monks and 4184 priests[11] were massacred
by the Republicans, and 50 churches burned down in Madrid in the
space of a single night, then it is hardly surprising that he came to see
fascism in its various forms as the lesser of two evils.

Only twenty-five years later, at the first session of Vatican II, how
different the signs of the times must have seemed. The fascist
dictators had been defeated and deposed; their rule replaced in
Western Europe by Christian Democrats, inspired by the teaching of
the Church. When, on July 8th, 1962, General de Gaulle and
Chancellor Adenauer attended mass together in Rheims Cathedral, it
showed how the old rivalry between France and Germany which had
bedevilled Europe for 150 years had been dissolved by the solidarity
of these two Catholic leaders.

Moreover, the old European empires which had subjected so many
in Africa and Asia were ending; there was peace in Algeria and the war
in Vietnam had not got under way. Even in Russia, under Khrushchev,
Stalin had been denounced and the Bolshevik state pledged to
peaceful coexistance. It was not a world without dangers but one in
which the signs of the times seemed to augur well.

It is common today to describe the opening sessions of the Council
as a struggle between liberals and conservatives in which the liberals
triumphed. Reading the decrees of the Council, it seems more
accurate to describe what difference there was between conservatives
and arch-conservatives. As a Protestant observer, Dr. Edward Norman, has noted , 'its reformulations of faith were, in the event,
surprisingly unitary and conservative'[12.]. Even when it came to the

liturgy, where change was most marked, the Council itself only *permitted* the vernacular; and Communion in both kinds was to be the exception, not the rule. The liturgy was 'the summit toward which the activity of the Church was directed'[13]; and the mass was confirmed as the perpetuation of 'the sacrifice of the Cross throughout the ages' [14]

In *Lumen Gentium* the Church was defined as 'the People of God' but *vox populi* was not *vox dei*. The People of God were not only to be be guided by the *magisterium*, they were to obey it; for it was not 'the mere word of men, but truly the word of God, the faith once and for all delivered to the saints'.[15] It also confirmed the power of the Pope.

> In order that the episcopate itself...might be one and undivided [Christ] put Peter at the head of the other apostles, and in him set up a lasting and visible source and foundation of the unity both of the faith and communion. This teaching concerning the institution, the permanence, the nature and the sacred primacy of the Roman Pontiff and his infallible teaching office, the sacred synod proposes anew to be believed by all the faithful.[16]

Nor was this submission to be limited to the dogmas pronounced *ex cathedra* of which there have anyway been few.

> This loyal submission of the will and intellect must be given, in a special way, to the authentic teaching authority of the Roman Pontiff even when he does not speak *ex cathedra* in such wise, indeed, that his supreme teaching authority be acknowledged with respect, and sincere assent be given to decisions made by him, conformably with his manifest mind and intention, which is made known principally either by the character of the documents in question, or by the frequency with which a certain doctrine is proposed, or by the manner in which the doctrine is formulated. [17]

The decree on Religious Liberty affirmed the sovereignty of the individual conscience, but this was not, as is often suggested, something new. 'The Catholic in his moral life,' wrote the German theologian, Karl Adam, in 1929,

> has only one subjective law, and that is his conscience. So that if a

divine ordinance be not plain and evident to his conscience, or if he be in a state of invincible error, then the Catholic is not bound by the objective law... In the last resort, the decisive factor in all matters which concern his faith or morals or in any wise determine his religious attitude, is the preeminence of conscience.[18]

This teaching was reiterated in the decree on Religious Liberty: no one should be coerced or cajoled into the Catholic Church. Man's response to God by faith must be free. However the preamble to the Decree is a statement of the freely arrived at belief of the Council fathers: 'We believe that [the] one true religion continues to exist in the Catholic and Apostolic Church'[19]; and ends with the admonition that those who consider themselves Catholics, in forming their consciences, must pay careful attention to the sacred and certain teaching of the Church. 'For the Catholic Church is by the will of Christ the teacher of truth'.

It was the same when it came to the decree on Other Religions and the Church's Missionary Activity: the Council recognised 'all that is true and holy in these religions... Yet she proclaims and is in duty bound to proclaim without fail, Christ who is the way, the truth and the life.' So too, in the decree on Ecumenism, it was stated that 'it is through Christ's Catholic Church alone, which is the universal help towards salvation, that the fullness of the means of salvation can be obtained.'[20]

The principal object of the decree on Ecumenism seems to have been, not to abolish or even overlook those dogmas and formulations of faith which divided the different Christian religons, but to do away with the *enmity* which had existed between them and accept what they had in common — above all, their baptism in Christ. Christians of other denominations should be accepted 'with respect and affection as brothers';[21] but even Cardinal Bea, the 'apostle of Ecumenism' who became President of the Secretariat for Christian Unity, regarded as

a point of fundamental importance, which no contact with our separated brethren must let us forget, *our adherence to the truth of our faith,* as contained in Holy Scripture and Catholic tradition, and presented to us by the teaching authority of the Church, must be *complete and unconditional*. No approach to our separated brethren, no work for union, must ever weaken that absolute adherence. So when we talk of greater respect and understanding between Catholics and non-Catholics, there is no question of adopting their outlook or their faith.[22]

The Council, too, taught that ecumenical activity must be 'fully and sincerely Catholic, that is, loyal to the truth we have received from the Apostles and the fathers, and in harmony with the faith which the Catholic Church has always professed...'[23] and warned Catholics against 'frivolous or imprudent zeal, for these can cause harm to true progress towards unity.'

The decree which was to have the most radical effect upon the *political* attitudes of Catholics was *Gaudium et spes*, the Pastoral Constitution on the Church in the Modern World. It is in this that we find the levelling of the ramparts which had surrounded the church since the Reformation, and their transformation into the tree-lined boulevards of the optimistic urban planner.

No longer is the world to be seen simply as the province of the Devil and life as a vale of tears. Man might have fallen but he was not all bad. For that reason the Council, 'in proclaiming the noble destiny of man and affirming an element of the divine in him', offered to cooperate unreservedly with mankind in 'fostering a sense of brotherhood to correspond to this destiny of theirs'. 'Ours is a new age of history', with an enormous potential for both good and bad.

The pace of change is so far-reaching and rapid nowadays that no one can allow himself to close his eyes to the course of events or indifferently ignore them and wallow in the luxury of a merely individualistic morality. The best way to fulfil one's obligations to justice and love is to contribute to the common good according to one's means and needs of others, even to the point of fostering and helping the public and private organisations devoted to bettering the conditions of life. There is a kind of person who boasts of grand and noble sentiments and lives in practice as if he could not care less about the needs of society. There are many in various countries who make light of social laws and directives and are not ashamed to resort to fraud and cheating to avoid paying just taxes and fulfilling other social obligations. There are others who neglect the norms of social conduct, such as those regulating public hygene and speed limits, forgetting that they are endangering their own lives and the lives of others in their carelessness.[24]

The hope expressed in this document that, with the help of God's grace there would arise 'a generation of new men, the moulders of a new humanity', who would keep the speed limit and pay their taxes, was nevertheless tempered by a trace of the Church's ancient misgivings. These lead to certain contradictions. For example the decree uses the word 'world' in two different senses; on the one hand 'the world which the Council has in mind is the whole human family seen in the context of everything which envelops it'; but on the other, it reminds us that in the Bible the world 'means a spirit of vanity and malice whereby human activity, from being ordered to the service of God and even man, is distorted to an instrument of evil'. [25]

It was also in something of a quandary about capitalism; for while the covetous instincts which inspired it are surely wrong, the very economic growth which it had brought about was the prerequisite to an improvement in people's standard of living. No longer was involuntary poverty to be seen as a 'privilege' as it had been by St. Francis of Sales[26] at a time when the gross world product was more or less static. Thus, while it talks of the many instances in which 'there exists a pressing need to reassess economic and social structures'[27] and says that 'every effort must be made to put an end as soon as possible to the immense economic inequalities which exist in the world and increase from day to day'[28], it does not specify, as came to be suggested, a socialist solution, talking of 'the role of 'every person concerned — owners, employers, management, and employees...''[29]

Indeed it is quite possible to glean from the decrees of *Gaudium et Spes* an endorsement of popular capitalism. 'When men and women provide for themselves and their families in such a way as to be of service to the community as well, they can rightly look upon their work as a prolongation of the work of the creator...' 'Private property or some form of ownership of external goods assures a person a highly necessary sphere for the exercise of his personal and family autonomy and ought to be considered an extension of human freedom'[30] This could have been written by Hayek, and legitimises policies like tax relief on mortgage interest and incentives for the wider ownership of shares.

Gaudium et Spes also warned Catholics, in their zeal to promote social justice and an amelioration in the condition of the poor, against forgetting the primary teaching of the Gospel. They 'must be careful to distinguish earthly progress clearly from the increase of the kingdom of Christ'[31]: 'Christ did not bequeath to the Church a mission in the political, economic or social order: the purpose he assigned to it was a religious one'.[32] It warned that 'unheavals in the social order' could come from 'selfishness and pride' as well as economic, political and social tensions[33] and that even where there was 'a pressing need to reassess economic and social structure...caution must be exercised with regard to the proposed solutions which may be untimely, especially those which offer material advantage while militating against man's spiritual nature and advancement. For "Man does not live by bread alone but by every word that comes from the mouth of God"'.[34]

The Post-conciliar Church

Given this tempered encouragement of social reform, which followed closely in spirit the Encyclical *Rerum Novarum* published by Pope Leo XIII in 1891, it is difficult to understand how *Gaudium et Spes*, together with the decrees on Religous Liberty and on Ecumenism, led to the turmoil in the Roman Catholic Church which has continued to this day.

The most telling statistic is that over the two decades which followed, 50,000 priests left the priesthood, with or without a dispensation from their vows. It has been suggested[35] that a truer estimate of departures world-wide for this period would be double that number. There was a comparable defection among nuns. For this, some conservatives blame the Council itself. To the former Archbishop of Dakar, Mgr Levebvre, 'it was the greatest disaster not only of this century but of any century since the foundations of the Church'.[36]

These upheavals took place largely during the painful pontificate of Pope Paul VI. Others[37] have described his dismay as the decrees which had been intended to trim the branches were used to lay an axe to the roots of the Church, a dismay which was to turn to anguish after his publication of *Humanae Vitae*, the encyclical on birth control.

The pithiest expression of the change in Catholic attitudes came from the novelist David Lodge who said that around 1970 Catholics ceased to believe in Hell. Not only did the laity cease to behave as if there was a credible danger of damnation but the clergy ceased to preach it. Yet one can hardly question that the New Testament teaches the existence of Hell — there are more than a dozen references to it in the gospel of St. Matthew alone; or that many of Christ's parables contain dire warnings of the fate which awaits those who die unrepentant — this despite the there were doubts about an afterlife among the Saducee Jews of his time.

Here, as we shall see, it is possible to see the influence of American values in the consciousness of post-war Catholics — the tendency to hide the more disagreeable facts of life like insanity, disease and death; and now the more disagreeable facts of the afterlife as well. Since Purgatory, too, had been rejected by the Protestant reformers, and therefore became an obstacle to the merger of the Christian churches, that too was dropped in the wake of Vatican II.

The paradox here is that in Auschwitz and Hiroshima, man in the twentieth century had more vivid paradigms of Hell than his predecessors; and it is perhaps a valid criticism of the Council that it made only implicit references to Hell which by necessity is at the core of Christian teaching. It does not seem to have intended to play it down; but nor does it dwell upon what awaits the unrepentant sinner; and this neglect was seized upon by a whole generation as an excuse for removing that fear of damnation which until then, particulary in the sphere of sexual morality, had determined how far they could go. Indeed the phenomenon of the post-Conciliar revolt among Catholics against the authority of the Church's teaching is paralled by that change in the mores of the Western World known as the sexual revolution.

The Sexual Revolution

Until this point, the Church's restrictive teaching on marriage and sexual morality had been supported by the link between sexual intercourse and the birth of a child. Since the child required nurture and protection, and since women required a husband to provide it, the religious ideal had a strong practical justification.

Economic and technical developments in the industrialised world, however, meant that by the time of the Council these practical supports had been removed. Prosperity released the energies man had usually expended on his struggle to survive; efficient mechanical methods of contraception broke the link between intercourse and conception; and the growth of industrial techniques which enabled women to do the work of men, as well as the extensive provision of both protection and welfare by the state, meant that women were to some extent freed from their dependence on men.

To Catholics during this period — many of whom were only Catholics because they had been born into Catholic families and raised to follow Catholic norms — it was one thing to endure the ridicule of rationalists for their absurd superstitions, but quite another to miss out on the fun simply to avoid a notional torment in a world that may or may not come.

The last straw came with the publication of *Humanae Vitae* two years after the end of the Council, the Encyclical of Pope Paul VI condemning the use of artificial methods of birth control. Since it was known that a majority of the commission advising the Pope on the matter had recommended a change in the Church's traditional teaching, and since majorities were now expected to have their way, there was a widespread disobedience to this Papal teaching and, as a consequence, a campaign which is sustained to this day, to reduce the status of the Papal Encyclical to no more than the private opinion of the Bishop of Rome.

After all, had not *Gaudium et spes* described sexual love as 'noble and honorable', and said that it was not just for the procreation of children? Ignoring the fact that the same decree had condemned 'unlawful contraceptive practices'[38] and had referred, albeit in a footnote, to Pius XI's uncompromising Encyclical, *Castii Conubii,* it was put about that Pope Paul had somehow gone back on the Council's intentions and could therefore safely be ignored.

The irony, of course, is that the very voices raised against Pope Paul's supposed demeaning of human sexuality were loudest in those countries like Holland, England or the United States, where the dominant Protestants had formerly condemned the Catholic countries of southern Europe for *tolerance* of the sins of the flesh. Thus we find, once again, the influence of the Anglo-Saxon victors of World War II.

Certainly, there had always been a prophetic mistrust of sexual love in Christian thinking. St. Augustine thought that original sin was a sexual sin: the first consequence of the Fall was the shame they both felt at their nakedness. In the Old Testament, Baal, the god of fertility, was Yahweh's great rival and the faithlessness of the adultress was equated with the faithlessness of the apostate. Illicit love led both David and Sampson astray; the very language of the Bible links innocence to virginity and corruption to carnal knowledge. Mary was a virgin; Christ was celibate; and St. Paul taught that while it was good to marry it was better to remain single.

Since it is said by some feminist theologians[39] that Church's interference with the morality of the marriage bed was the invention of celibate men, it should be remembered that St. Catherine of Sienna saw, in her vision of the damned, many souls grievously tormented for having violated the sanctity of marriage 'which happened, said she, not for the enormity of the sin, for murders and blasphemies are more enormous, but because they that commit it make no conscience of it and therefore continue long in it.'[40]

This distinction between Catholic and Protestant cultures, then, is not a difference about what is sinful but about what we do about the sin. To the Catholic, life is a continuous cycle of sin and repentance leading, with the help of the Grace of God and by the persistent effort of the sinner, to eventual sanctity and salvation. To the Protestant, however, who accepts the Lutheran or Calvinist concept of predestination, a man is either saved or he is not. If he is saved, he will not sin or, to the Antinomian, what he does cannot be considered a sin. Thus, for example, when the Americans — a people affected more than they realize by the ideology of the Puritan founders of their nation — are told by Kinsey that most of them masturbate, their reaction is not to repent but to conclude that if everyone does it, it cannot be wrong.

The spread of American influence after World War II is not to be measured just by the advance of jeans and Coca Cola, but by the acceptance of concepts such as 'self-evident' human rights; the pursuit of happiness as an ideal; of pluralism, democracy and many of those other ideas which were viewed with such suspicion by the Popes in the nineteenth century. It is to be traced in the decrees of Vatican II, and triumphed in the repudiation of *Humanae Vitae* which itself dared to reject not just the American technology of the contraceptive pill but Hollywood's idea of sex as the expression of romantic love.

To those in the Third World, where marriage, which was often arranged, was seen in a more practical light, the teaching of *Humanae Vitae* matched peoples' moral intuiton; but it is another paradox of the Council, which intended to end the dominance of Europeans in the life of the Church, that it has in fact been used to justify the export of European and North American intellectual fads like consumerism and liberation theology. From contraception springs the contraceptive mentality which presents sex as a consumer's indulgence — a mixed sensual, social and sportive encounter. Biologically speaking, after all, the condom is the functional equivalent of the Romans' *vomitorium* and its ubiquity is symptomatic of a culture of indulgence.

The most valid criticism which can be made of the Church over the issue of contraception, and this applies to the question of abortion too, is that an emphasis first on one aspect (contraception), and then on one consequence (abortion), of sexual sin has obscured the overall virtue of chastity, the name given by the Church not so much to abstinence as to innocence and sincerity in sexual love.

The word 'chastity' today, like 'virginity', 'purity' or 'modesty', has become abhorrent: even many who are Catholic and want to be good, do not aspire to be holy. They may agree that adultery is wrong, and intend to be faithful to their husbands or wives, but they rebel against the idea that there can be sexual sin within a marriage, or that their fantasy should be subject to the moral law.

Yet if they are honest they will acknowledge that bad conscience *can* enter into conjugal love because, as Gustav Thibon wrote, 'the sexual instinct can never operate in its simple animalism: it must rise above or fall below it. Unless it climbs up towards God, or it must drop down to the devil. If it is not *love*, it becomes *lust*.'[41] Particularly in the urban communities of the developed world, the erotic propaganda through television, advertising and cinema can lead married couples to pursue an elusive sexual fulfilment long after both the procreative and unitive functions of their marriage are accomplished. As Simone de Beauvoir appreciated, the essential character of eroticism is 'a movement towards the Other', yet where a marriage is successful 'husband and wife become for one another the Same'.

> Thus if they do continue to make love, it is often with a sense of shame; they feel that the sexual act is no longer an intersubjective experience in which each goes beyond self, but rather a kind of joint masturbation. That they each regard the other as a utensil necessary for the satisfaction of their needs is a fact that conjugal politeness ignores but that springs to view if this politeness fails.[42]

Nor are sins against chastity only acts; they can be committed in the imagination. No sin is more ridiculed today than that of 'impure thoughts' which used to be whispered through the grill of the confessional; yet it was not some prurient Pope but Christ himself who warned that 'if a man looks at a woman lustfully, he has already committed adultery with her in his heart'; and then added, 'If your eye should cause you to sin, tear it out and throw it away; for it will do you less harm to lose one part of you than to have your whole body thrown into hell.'[43]

All this was vehemently rejected by the articulate Catholics after publication of *Humanae Vitae*. Its teaching was repudiated publicly by Catholic priests and led some, like the Jesuit John F X Harriott, to leave first his order, then the priesthood and finally get married. Many liberated Catholics among the laity, influenced by Freud and D H Lawrence, came to see sexual repression as a serious sin. Good sex led to personal fulfilment and personal fulfilment was a human right. Even the clergy who remained true to their vows often preferred to avoid, when they could, the question of contraception. Many became afraid to promote chastity with much zeal, or condemn such classic sexual sins as sodomy, masturbation and 'so-called free love'[44].

It is only now that we can see that contraception has not delivered what it promised. Abortion was to become redundant: there are now, in Britain, around 200,000 abortions a year. There were to be no more children born out of wedlock: in the decades since the Encyclical they have risen from one in twenty to one in four. The rise in venereal disease, heart disease, and cervical cancer in younger women, have all been ascribed to the contraceptive pill, or to the start of sexual relations at an early age. An increase in sterility in women comes frequently from gynaecological disease and condoms are now recommended not so much to prevent conception as contraction of AIDS.

The other development, which *Gaudium et spes* had described as a 'plague', was the dramatic increase in divorce. Between 1960 and 1987 in England and Wales the number of divorces per annum increased sixfold, and it is now estimated that in future more than half of all marriages will end in divorce. Into these statistics can be read not just a wholesale rejection of the Christian teaching that marriage should be a commitment for life, but an astonishing indifference to the acute and lasting suffering of children whose families are ruptured by their parents separation.

The causes for the rise in divorce are varied, but the idea put forward in the 1960s that a less rigid code of sexual ethics would lead ultimately to more stable unions has been disproved by experience. Indeed in America it has been established that 'there is a clear inverse correlation between pre-marital cohabitation', or 'trial marriage', and later marital stability: 'those whose marriages were preceded by a period of cohabition are *more* likely to divorce quickly than those who did not live together before marriage'.[45] Much of what was predicted by Pius XI in his Encyclical *Castii Conubii*, which so embarrassed the progressive theologians at the time of the Council, seems to have come to pass.

The reason given by Laurence Stone, the historian of marriage and divorce, for the rapid spread of divorce over the past twenty years are 'the increasingly pervasive ideologies of individualism, the pursuit of personal happiness and the expectation of relatively speedy gratification' and the disintegration of the family as an integrated economic unit as women go out to work. 'It is no accident,' he writes, 'that the divorce rate has risen concurrently with the influx of married women into the labour market'; and 'the egalitarian ideology of feminism has had a major impact'.[46]

Feminism

From the time of Christ until World War II the Church had had a clear and consistent teaching on question of women. Both Leo XIII Encyclical *Arcanum* in 1880 and Pius XI's *Casti Connubii* in 1930 drew confidently from the writing of both St. Paul and St. Augustine to confirm not just the norms of sexual morality, but also primacy of the husband over his wife and children.

> The husband is the ruler of the family and the head of the wife; but the wife, because she is flesh of his flesh and bone of his bone, will submit to him and obey him, not as a servant but as a companion; and thus her

obedience will not be wanting in either honour and dignity.[47]

Among 'the errors concerning marriage' denounced by Pius XI — 'if the enemy's wiles are to be foiled they must first be exposed' — was 'the emancipation of woman'.

> The same false teachers, who by the spoken and the written word seek to dim the lustre of marital fidelity and chastity, attack also the loyal and honourable obedience of the wife to her husband, which some of them even describe as an ignominious servitude of one partner to the other. All rights between husband and wife, they say, are equal, and since the servitude of one of the partners is a violation of this equality, they blatently proclaim or demand the emancipation of woman...

To 'free the wife from the domestic cares of children and family, enabling her, to the neglect of these, to follow her own bent and engage in business and even in public affairs' he denounced as

> a degradation of the spirit of woman and of the dignity of a mother; it is a total perversion of family life, depriving the husband of his wife, the children of their mother and the home and the family of their ever-watchful guardian. The wife herself cannot but suffer damage from this unnatural equality with her husband.[48]

When Vatican II convened in 1962, no women were to be found among its auditors or theological advisers. After a complaint by Cardinal Suenens that 'half of the Church was excluded', some women were appointed as auditors and worked on the drafting of the decree on the Laity and the Church in the Modern World. As a result it encourages women's 'participation in cultural life' and their 'legitimate social advancement'[49].

Pius XI, too, had acknowledged that 'the changed circumstances and customs of human intercourse may render necessary some modification in the social and economic condition of the married woman' and called upon 'the public authority to adapt the civil rights of the wife to the needs and requirements of modern times'; but where he insisted that 'the essential order of the home' remain inviolate,

Gaudium et Spes merely recongises that 'the mother...has a central role to play in the home, for the children, especially the younger children, depend on her considerably'.[50]

In Pope John XXIII's Encyclical *Pacem in Terris* of April, 1965, he recognised further that 'since women are becoming ever more conscious of their human dignity, they will not tolerate being treated as mere material instruments, but demand rights befitting a human person in both domestic and public life'. If he thought this would placate the growing body of Christian feminists, he was mistaken. As Ronald Knox noted in his book *Enthusiasm*, 'from the Montanist movement onwards, the history of enthusiasm is largely a history of female emancipation, and it is not a reassuring one'.[51]

Not content with the Church's encouragement to secure equal rights in civil society, the growing band of feminists within the Church demanded equal rights within the Church too — including the right to be ordained as priests. In 1976 Franjo Cardinal Seper, then the Prefect of the Sacred Congregation for the Doctrine of the Faith, pronounced that for a variety of reasons women could never be ordained as priests. 'The Incarnation of the Word took place according to the male sex; this is indeed a question of fact, and this fact, while not implying an alleged natural superiority of man over woman, cannot be disassociated from the economy of salvation.'[52] However, this did not prevent — indeed it probably encouraged — the ordination of women becoming an article of faith among the progressive theologians.

While on the question of birth control the Church has nailed its colours to the mast, it remains defensive when faced with feminism; even Pope John Paul II in *Mulieris Dignitatem* neither accepted nor repudiated the teaching on the question of his predecessor, Pius XI; yet the scriptural foundation for the traditional teaching would appear to be far stronger than that which underpins the teaching of *Humanae Vitae*. The more one ponders the ancient, priestly, version of creation in Genesis, the more it is seen as the source of truth about the bond between the sexes. Far from suggesting an ignominious subjection of woman to man, it presents woman as God's most precious gift to man, a gift of man's choosing and one which he acclaimed. To reject her, exchange her or misuse her becomes an act of gross ingratitude to God.

However, a significance is given to the primary creation of Adam by St. Paul which is inimical to feminism. It is man who 'is the image of God's glory,' wrote St. Paul in his first letter to the Corinthians, 'whereas a woman reflects the glory of man. For man did not originally spring from woman, but woman was made out of man; and man was not created for woman's sake, but woman for the sake of man...'[53] This hierarchy was part of the proper order of the world, and just as Christ obeyed God, the Church must obey Christ, a man must obey the Church and a woman her husband. 'Wives should regard their husbands as they regard the Lord, since as Christ is head of the church and saves the whole body, so is the husband the head of his wife; and as the Church submits to Christ, so should wives to their husbands, in everything'.[54]

Nor was it just within marriage that women were to play a subordinate role. 'I am not giving permission,' St. Paul wrote to St. Timothy, 'for a woman to teach or to tell a man what to do. A woman ought not to speak, because Adam was formed first and Eve afterwards...'[55] Nor was St. Paul the only apostle to believe that wives should be submissive: St. Peter, too, wrote that 'wives should be obedient to their husbands'[56]; but neither St. Peter nor St. Paul were authorising the chattel status that is accorded to women in so many other religions of the world. 'Husbands love your wives and treat them with gentleness,' wrote St. Paul to the Colossians; and again, to the Ephesians, 'husbands must love their wives as they love their own bodies'; and St. Peter insisted that husbands 'must always treat their wives with consideration in their life together, respecting a woman as one who, though she may be the weaker partner, is equally an heir to the life of grace'.[57]

To the feminists in the post-Conciliar period, the unambiguous teaching of the two founders of the Church presented a difficulty; for while it was possible, and common, to denigrate St. Paul as a misogynist, it was hardly possible to deny his *authority* without undermining the theological edifice upon which the whole Church was built.

Vatican II, after all, whose decrees were so necessary to the progressive theologians in their reformulation of Catholic belief, was peppered with quotations from St. Paul. However, there was, in the decree on Divine Revelation a clause which allowed biblical scholars to 'look for that meaning which the sacred writers, in a determined situation and given circumstances of his time and culture, intended to express and did in fact express, through the medium of a contemporary literary form.'[58]

This enabled the Dutch Dominican, Edward Schillebeeckx, to decide that St. Paul' teaching on women, although based upon Genesis, was merely giving

> a theological superstructure to a factual situation which was reflected in the household codes and was accepted as a human ethos — the situation of the wife's subjection to her husband — and to the generally inferior and secondary position of women in society, and that he did this by referring to the second and older Genesis account of the creation in which the assertion of the woman's subordinate position was itself a reflection of an actual social situation'.[59]

Now, while Fr. Schillebeeckx is a celebrated theologian, not least because he has been censored by the Holy Office in Rome, and I am no theologian at all, it needs only common sense to see that this method can be used to negate any or all of the Church's teaching — in particular that on marriage which comes from Genesis and is the cornerstone of the Christian concept of sexual morality. It also overlooks Christ's specific endorsement of the authority of Genesis when he superseded Moses on the question of divorce.

> Have you not read that the creator from the beginning *made them male and female* and that he said: *This is why a man must leave father and mother, and cling to his wife, and the two become one body.* They are no longer two, therefore, but one body. So, then, what God has united,

man must not divide.[60]

Moreover, there is a consistency on the question of women which runs from the time of Abraham to the publication of *Castii Conubii* in 1930 which would suggest that Fr Schillebeeckx to prove his point would have to establish that some elemental change occurred in human nature between 1930 and the present day.

It may be thought that the feminist challenge is unimportant; that because of some genuine prejudice against women, and the absurd masculine arrogance to be found in posturing, immature men, that men of good will should placate the Feminists by promoting them in the lay structures of the Church and allowing them to propogate their ideas through catechetical courses used in Catholic schools; but just as the failure to preach chastity with any vigour has led to a great increase in the suffering of children, so too women themselves have suffered from feminism.

For if woman is not God's aboriginal gift to man, then he is free to take her or leave her as he chooses; to prefer a helpmate of his own sex; to trade her in for a younger woman; to leave her to fend for herself. 'Up to now,' writes Ivan Illich, 'whenever equal rights were legally enacted and enforced...the innovation gave a sense of accomplishment to the elites who proposed and obtained them, but left the majority of women untouched, if not worse off than before.'[61] The 'liberation' of women has invariably meant adding a job in a factory or office to the work they already did in the home.

Feminism has harmed marriage, too, not just in contributing to divorce as I have shown above, but by destroying the harmony of family life. 'All my clinical experience,' wrote the marriage therapist A C Robin Skynner,

> extending now over more than twenty years, has certainly convinced me that, other things being equal, the optimal pattern for family functioning is one in which the father in general accepts the ultimate responsibility and the authority which goes with this. That is, in seeking ways to improve the functioning of families, in order to relieve distresses complained of or achieve satisfactions desired, I have found

that problems have been regularly associated with a relative inadequacy of the father to exercise leadership or management functions, and a corresponding overactivity of the mother in the parental 'decider subsystem'. A change in the relative activity or ultimate responsiblity towards the father's side has been an essential component in attaining the family's stated goals, including the mothers. I have also been struck by the way this view is so widely shared throughout the literature on family therapy, sometimes explicitly, more often implicitly in case examples (some North American therapists have told me they avoid expressing such views openly in the present climate of opinion).[62]

The Alternative Magisterium

The quotation a few pages back from Schillebeeckx on the question of St. Paul's teaching on women gives a flavour of the way in which influential theologians, instead of serving the Church's teaching, interpret it to fit an egalitarian ideology of secular derivation. This 'parallel' or 'alternative *magisterium*' has been developed since Vatican II and is held by its protagonists to be as valid, if not more valid, than the teaching of the Congregation for the Doctrine of the Faith, or even the Pope, in Rome. There are even areas within the Church where it has become an intolerant orthodoxy, excommunicating anyone who rejects it as surely as the ancient inquisition. 'Traditional' Catholics, while not burned at the stake, are subjected a 'soft' persecution — condemned as reactionary if they are theolgians; written off as 'burnt-out' if they are priests; and labelled 'unsuitable' for the priesthood if they are seminarians.

Counting on the awe before 'science' which is found in the secular world, the progressive theologians suggest that they are privy to 'discoveries' which the untutored cannot expect to understand. In contrast to the clarity, brevity and simplicty of the New Testament, their works are voluminous and opaque. The suggestion of Karl Rahner, for example, that God is to be found in man becomes, in theologese, the establishment of 'the transcendental character of human subjectivity as a constitutive moment of revelation', or the 'ambitious image of the co-naturality of the Creature and the creature, dynamically orientated towards one another.'[63]

Fundamental to the claims to authority of the alternative *magisterium* is the premise that theology is a science like any other which 'progresses' towards the truth over the years. But as Lord Macaulay pointed out

> Natural theology...is not a progressive science... But neither is revealed religion of the nature of a progressive science. All Divine truth is...recorded in certain books. It is equally open to all who, in any age, can read those books; nor can all the discoveries of all the philosophers in the world add a single verse to any of these books. It is plain, therefore, that in divinity there cannot be a progress analagous to that which is constantly taking place in pharmacy, geology, and navigation.[64]

Undoubtedly theology, over the centuries, has contributed towards the development of Church's doctrine, and Christians' understanding of their faith but, though it has been called the queen of sciences, it is in fact the mere handmaid of religion — as superfluous to sanctity as the study of aesthetics is to the creation of a work of art. 'Lofty words do not make a man just or holy,' wrote Thomas à Kempis, 'but a good life makes him dear to God. I would rather feel contrition than be able to define it. If you know the whole Bible by heart, and all the teachings of the philosophers, how could this help you without the grace and love of God?'[65]; or, as Christ himself put it in St. Luke's Gospel, 'I bless you, Father, Lord of heaven and of earth, for hiding these things from the learned and the clever and revealing them to mere children.'[66]

However, the modern theologian would make mincemeat of quotations from Lord Macauley, Thomas à Kempis or even Christ. At its most extreme, modern Catholic theology accepts the premises of two theories which became fashionable in the decades following Vatican II — Marxism and Structuralism. Following the structuralists, doubt is cast upon our understanding of words written in other eras. Meanings change, so Scripture, Papal Encyclicals and Council Decrees cannot be assumed to mean what they say. We must work out what was meant, and express it in contemporary terms. Only theologians, of course, are competent to do this.

Yet even theologians, it is conceded, are but human: they too use contemporary language, and are conditioned in their thinking by the prejudices of their *milieu*, which in turn serve the interests of the dominant class. Thus, theological theories interact with political points of view; since history is progressing towards a socialist millenium, the establishment of the Kingdom of Heaven becomes linked to the Marxist vision of world revolution and the triumph of the working class.

This 'liberation' theology is at the heart of the alternative *magisterium*. Posited as a theology of the Third World, and tracing its pedigree to a meeting of young theologians at Petropolis in Brazil in 1964, it is reminiscent of earlier quasi-Marxist movements in the Church such as that of the French worker priests, and is largely the brainchild of European and South American theologians, many of whom studied European universities like Louvain.[67]

Taking its key from the Vatican II decrees of *Gaudium et spes* calling for an improvement in the material condition of the poor, it secured its first triumph in Medellin in 1968 when the Bishops of South America declared their 'preferential option for the poor'. This was interpreted by the 'progressive' or 'popular' church as episcopal approval for its collective, political, largely material and often Marxist and revolutionary concept of salvation. The high point for the *praxis* of this theology was the successful Sandinista revolution in Nicaragua: two priests became ministers in the government. An attempt at a repeat performance in neighbouring El Salvador has led to ten years of civil war and more than 70,000 deaths.

The basic objection to Liberation Theology is that it reverses the priorities of the Christian life, denying the 'invisible realities', subordinating the divine to the human, contemplation to action, and positing a paradise in this world, not in 'that city yet to come'.[68] The supernatural dimension is discounted if not denied. Salvation is not from Hell but from political oppression and social injustice; liberation is not from sin but from the sinful structures of authoritarian regimes. The Eucharist is no longer a reenactment of Christ's sacrifice in the mass, but a meal symbolising the unity of the people. Indeed Christ is no longer the Son of God who died for our sins, but an exemplary figure who fought for the poor like Sandino or Farabundo Marti.

In its favour it should be said of Liberation Theology that it has helped make Christians aware of the dire poverty of most of those who live in the Third World, and has inspired many to try and do something about it. Prosperous Christians cannot but be haunted by the words of Christ in St Matthew's gospel: 'Go away from me, with your curse upon you, to eternal fire prepared for the devil and his angels. For I was hungry and you never gave me food; I was thirsty, and you never gave me anything to drink.'[69]

However, the Liberation Theologians, rather than simply shedding what wealth they themselves possess, appear more intent upon expropriating the wealth of others. Just as the Communists made a God of the working class to justify taking political power by force, so the liberationists make a God of 'the poor'. By accepting a Marxist analysis of history, and cooperating in practice with those who believe that violent revolution was the only solution to endemic poverty in the Third World, Liberation Theology has become a narrow ideology that cannot adapt itself to changing circumstances or to the unpalatable paradoxes of reality.

In El Salvador, for example, many of the Catholics in base communities who followed its teaching committed themselves to support the Marxist guerillas, the FMLN. Undoubtedly the government in El Salvador was at one time undemocratic and elements of the Armed Forces remain brutal and uncontrolled: they were undoubtedly behind the murder of Archbishop Romero in 1979, and of the five Jesuits, their housekeeper and her daughter ten years later. It is indisputable, too, that much of the land belongs to few of the people. It is also true, however, that the civil war, in destroying the substructure of the country and deterring foreign investment, has further impoverished those already poor. It is also a fact that where cooperatives have been tried they have not succeeded. It is also a fact that a large part of the country's national income comes from the United States, either as aid or as remittances from Salvadorians who work there, so that if this was lost as a result of a victory of the guerillas, the country would inevitably be still worse off than before.

This is recognised by those bishops in El Salvador who adhere to what is called the 'traditional' Church. The followers of Liberation Theology, led by the Jesuits of the University of Central America, and well represented in the Archdiocese of San Salvador, make up the 'progressive' Church. The traditionalists look to the Pope; the progressives to the memory of the assassinated archbishop Romero. To the traditionalists Romero was a good but gullible man who was manipulated by Marxist priests; to the progressives the Pope is the apostle of an 'oppressive' Christianity, a peddlar of an opiate Catholicism to the People of God. The progressives live in fear of the death squads; the traditionalists live in fear of the guerillas. 'The real untold story,' a Salesian father told me, 'is the persecution of the *traditional* church.'

From his point of view, the objection to Liberation Theology was not so much that it fuels the passions of a civil war, or in the name of development sets back the development of an impoverished country, but rather that, in order to use the Catholic Church to promote political objectives, it distorts the message of the Gospel; for it is quite apparent to even the most amateur exegete that the Jews in Palestine at the time of Christ were as oppressed by the Romans as any Third World country is by an America-backed oligarchy today, yet Christ pointedly refused to sanction any kind of political revolt. The things that are Caesar's were to be rendered unto Caesar: his kingdom was not of this world. When the Devil offered to turn stones into bread, which would have fed many hungry people, Christ resisted the temptation because 'man does not live by bread alone'.

Liberationists, it would appear, have fallen for this temptation and in their concern for man's social and material condition, have neglected the needs of his soul. As a result, not only are some Catholics distracted from their supernatural destiny, but many others, starved of a spiritual religion, turn to Pentecostalist and Evangelical sects which, though remote in their liturgy from the Apostolic Church, nonetheless preach a simple message of faith in Christ, repentance of sin, and salvation from damnation. In Central and South America, vast numbers who have grown tired of being told that they are poor and oppressed, and weary of suffering from revolutionary wars, have defected to the Pentecostalist and Evangelical churches. In Mexico, Guatamala and Peru a large proportion of the population are now Christians of a non-Catholic kind. The final paradox for progressive Catholics is this: that in a generation, if present trends continue, the poor will still be with them but they will no longer belong to the Catholic Church.

The British Liberationists

One advantage of the progressives is their network of supporters in other parts of the world. When I wrote an article critical of the progressive Church in El Salvador, I was criticised from the pulpit of the Jesuits' church in Mayfair. In London, as in San Salvador or Managua, the Liberationists are intolerant of views which are not their own. Ask if the Leninist leadership of the FMLN is not also undemocratic; or why, if socialism has failed in Eastern Europe, in should succeed elsewhere; or if capitalism in Western Europe has not improved the lot of the poor; or what lessons can be learnt from the prosperity of formerly impoverished countries in the Far East; or if the National Health Service which performs 200,000 abortions a year is not, by their definition, a more 'sinful structure' than the Salvadorian Armed Forces; and you are met with implacable enmity, not a reasoned reply.

In Britain the adherents of Liberation Theology appear to dominate most of the Church's lay institutions. The Catholic Institute for International Affairs (CIIR) which has the Rev. David Konstant, the Bishop of Leeds, as its Episcopal Adviser, unambiguously promotes its objectives. Running an Overseas Development Administration 90% of which is funded by the British government, and 18% spent on its UK administration, it has a separate programme of 'education' supported largely from religous agencies and Church sources such as the National Catholic Fund, money raised in parishes throughout England and Wales.

This puts out pamphlets and publications of an overtly partisan kind — Feminist, Liberationist, anti-capitalist, anti-American; and organises conference of the kind held in October, 1989, to discuss 'Oppressive Christianity in the Third Word', by which was meant not just the right-wing Evangelical sects which were making such inroads in the Third World, but also the Pope's episcopal appointments and the criticism of Liberation Theology by the Vatican.

Though purportedly Catholic and international, there is no mention whatsoever in either its catalogue or its review of any injustice perpetrated in Lithuania, Cuba, China, North Vietnam, or any nation under Communist control: nor is there room in their rogues' gallery beside Pinochet, DeKlerk and Christiani for socialist leaders like Ceausescu or Pol Pot.

The CIIR has close links with CAFOD, the Catholic Fund for Overseas Development, whose director, Julian Filochowski, sits on its Executive Committee, as does one of its three trustees, Mildred Neville. CAFOD'S address in London is 2 Romero Close and, although the bulk of its funds go to relieve hunger and encourage development in the Third World, it also contributes, for example, to the *Tutela Legal,* the legal department of the Archdiocese of San Salvador, which acts for catechists and members of base communities, many of them sympathetic to the FMLN.

If there is little scrutiny among Catholics of either CAFOD or the CIIR, it is because almost all the Catholic periodicals follow a similar line. *The Tablet*, an intelligent and well-edited weekly review, publishes in its section 'The Church in the World' items which read like press releases from the CIIR. CIIR conferences are covered by the former Jesuit, Michael Walsh, now Librarian at Heythrop College, the Theological Faculty of London University, who is a member of the Council of the CIIR. No one reading *The Tablet* could possibly suspect that the majority of the bishops in El Salvador, including the President of the Bishops Conference, the Bishop of Zacatecoluca, Monsignor Tovar, recognize the legitimacy of the Arena government and its armed forces, and condemn the FMLN.

The editorial line of *The Tablet* is not confined to favouring Liberation Theology; it invariably supports dissident theologians and criticises the 'official' church. It is opposed, in advance, to the Universal Catechism which is being prepared in Rome: on *Humanae Vitae*, homosexuality, women priests, married priests, Ecumenicism, intercommunion, and the full *table d' hote* of the alternative *magisterium* it faithfully reflects the progressive point of view. It is the same when it comes to the *Catholic Herald*, a paper even more zealous than *The Tablet* in opposing the Vatican and promoting the cause of the anti-capitalist 'progressive' Church.

There remains *The Universe*, the religious paper with the widest circulation in Britain and owned by the Bishops of England and Wales. What is its line? It is in favour of justice and peace. It against war. It is against poverty and famine and abortion too. Every now and then it will carry an insert promoting the 'progressive' church; but by and large it pursues a bland, inoffensive line reflecting a bland, inoffensive religion whose main purpose, like Oxfam or the Red Cross, is to help the hungry, the sick and the poor.

Weaving the Web

Not so bland is the 'modular programme of Religious Education' for Catholic secondary schools called *Weaving the Web* written by Richard Lohan and a graduate of Heythrop college, Sister Mary McClure, and published with the apparent approval of such ecclesiastical dignitaries as Monsignor David Konstant, the Bishop of Leeds and Episcopal adviser to CIIR; Monsignor Ralph Brown, the Vicar General of the Archdiocese of Westminster; and Monsignor Vincent Nichols, the Secretary to the Conference of Bishops of England and Wales, whose *Nihil Obstat* declares that the book is free from 'doctrinal or moral' error.

As the authors proudly announce, *Weaving the Web* is 'cumulatively systematic. As pupils work through the talks of each modular

theme, they are gradually being introduced, by a drip-feed process, to
the principal beliefs and practices of the major religous traditions...'
'Religious education is not *primarily* concerned with maturing and
developing Christian faith. Its aim is to help people to be aware of and
appreciate the religious dimension of life and they way this has been
expressed in religious tradition'.[70]

What is meant by this is revealed by a list in the Teacher's book of
what the pupil will know when he has finished level one.

> The pupil:
> 1.   Can identify a variety of groups.
> 2.   Recall experience of previous school.
> 3.   Knows about school patron.
> 4.   Knows what term 'third world' means.
> 5.   Knows where Latin America is.
> 6.   Knows that Baptism is a sign of initiation into the   Christian
> Community.'

By this same method of progressing unobtrusively from the unex-
ceptionable to the partisan, some of the enthusiasms of the alternative
magisterium are introduced into the pupil's mind.

Liberationism: Before Christ is even mentioned, the pupil will know
that 'there are great contrasts between the poor people who live in Peru
and the rich people who live there' and that 'In Peru most people are
very poor, and a small number of people are very rich'. They will also
know that Baptism 'is the sign of belonging to the Christian community', not that it washes away original sin.

Jesus is introduced as 'the founder of Christianity', 'for Christians...a
very important figure, the Son of God'. 'Jesus preached good news
about God's forgiveness. He preached to the poor. He said that God's
Kingdom belonged to the poor in spirit. Jesus was put to death for
what he preached'.[71] The juxtaposition of 'the poor' 'poor in spirit'
and 'was put to death for what he preached', coming after the data
about poverty in Peru, and its illustration by the story of two

Peruvians, one rich and one poor, helps the pupil to understand that 'The Eucharist is the sacrament of Liberation' or 'the celebration of Christian Freedom'[72]; to explore 'the image of Jesus as liberator'; and accept that Oscar Romero, Desmond Tutu and Martin Luther King are the prophetic figures of the modern world, rather than any of 20th century martyrs in Mexico, Spain, China or the USSR.

Thus Jesus is no longer the Paschal victim who died for the sins of all men, rich and poor alike, and save them from the torments of Hell; he becomes a kind of Che Guevara of the ancient world. Sanctity, it would seem, comes not from prayer, self-denial or sacramental grace but from political activism in the community. Sin is not offending God but 'missing the mark', and in giving absolution the priest does not 'act in the person of Christ the head'[73] but as 'representative of the community'. 'It's a way of saying sorry to everybody, including God, without making personal apologies to everyone in the community.'[74] One of the themes suggested for discussion are: 'are priests necessary?'

Ecumenism: The Church is not, following Vatican II, 'the society in the present world...governed by the successor of Peter and by the bishops in communion with him'[75]; instead

    the word CHURCH is used to refer to
        — the buildings where Christians worship
        — the Christian community locally
        — a Christian denomination
        — the world-wide Christian community

Pupils are asked to 'Make a list of all the christian churches which are around your school, or in the area where you live. They are all Christian, but they show that there are different families within the large Christian community which is called the church'.[76]

Syncretism (world religion): As promised by the authors, the pupil learns about all the world's major religious traditions - Islam, Hinduism, Judaism and Christianity; and so scrupulous are they to be fair to the non-Christian religions, that not only is Christianity denied pride of place, it is not presented as *true* in a way that the other religions are not.

The introduction of Christ as an historical person is prepared by a module called 'Story'. 'It is all about the stories that are told and written down by communities and individuals about the mystery of life'. First comes a Hindu story about the boyhood of Lord Krishna, then the story of Guru Nanak of the Sikhs, and finally the Bible which 'for Christians...is the WORD OF GOD'. Thus while the historicity of Jesus is not denied, he is given no greater standing than Lord Krishna.

If anything there is a bias in favour of non-Christian religions. In the module on slavery, we are told that 'many of the slave-traders were Christians'[77], not that they bought their slaves in Africa from Muslim Arabs, or that slavery was found in Islamic societies long after it had been abolished in the British empire, and is even said to exist in some Muslim countries today; or that the untouchables in Hindu society have a status every bit as demeaning as that of a slave.

Feminism: 'What do you think about the idea of women being priests?' the pupils are asked.[78] And they are told to

> Make a list of which jobs are done by which person in your family group. Are there any jobs which are always done by the female and any which are always done by the male members of the family group? Explain why this is so. Which jobs could be done by either sex? Write a poem or a short story where all the roles in the family group are reverse; perhaps you could call it "Equal Opportunities".[79]

A task called "Reflecting on Gender" is followed by another on "Prejudice and Discrimination"[80]. In a module on Roles and Responsibilities, there is an exchange between a peasant and a doctor in Peru. 'Does your wife work?' the doctor asks. 'No, she stays at home.'

There then follows a list of the labours of a wife in the third world, including taking lunch to her husband in the fields. `She has to walk about two miles...' `But you said your wife doesn't work?' `No. I told you. She stays at home'.[81]

Finally, in translating Genesis 1: 26-27 in a module entitled "Made in God's image", the usual translation: 'God said: Let us make man in our own image...' is given as 'God said: Let us make man and woman in our image...' And 'in the image of God he created him, male and female he created them...' is given as 'in the image of God, male and female, God created them.' This can be justified by the distinction to be made between man meaning male and man meaning mankind but, as we have seen, these verses of Genesis are pregnant with meaning.

It would be unjust to say that there is nothing good to be said for *Weaving the Web*; it apparently succeeds in arousing the interest of pupils in religion and, particularly in the later series, "Communication, Celebration, Values", there is evidence of some concession to a wider constituency within the Church — references, for example, to Lourdes, to Mother Teresa and to St Maximilian Kolbe. It is also true that the course is not meant to be catechesis, but as a programme of religious education.

The fact remains, however, that in both series Christianity is presented as just one among several other faiths, and the Catholic Church as just one branch of the Christian Church. And Christian belief is shown either as a blend of custom and folklore which has arisen out of 'the Christian community'; or as an ideology for the material development of impoverished countries in the Third World. Feminist propaganda is added for good measure.

No one, after studying *Weaving the Web*, could recognise the Catholic Church as it is described in Vatican II. And it is difficult to see how any Catholic child, after three years of its 'drip-feed process', could see any reason to be a Catholic rather than a Mormon, a Muslim or a Boy Scout.

Conclusion

'Among the more important duties of bishops,' said the decree *Lumen Gentium*, 'that of preaching the Gospel has pride of place. For the bishops are heralds of the faith, who draw new disciples to Christ; they are authentic teachers, that is, teachers endowed with the authority of Christ, who preach the faith ... they make it bear fruit and with watchfulness they ward off whatever errors threaten their flock'.[82]

The question posed by *Weaving the Web* is whether the Roman Catholic Bishops of England and Wales are performing this duty. Are they warding off errors which threaten their flock, or are they condoning a distortion of the Catholic Faith in schools which come under their jurisdiction? It is hard to tell. As the Church embarks upon the decade of Evangelisation, it is difficult to discover what the bishops themselves believe. In 1988, the very year in which *Weaving the Web* was first published, Cardinal Hume, the Archbishop of Westminster, addressed pilgrims from his diocese at Aylesford.

> Let me speak to you seriously about my own thoughts and concerns at this time. I have three priorities for my ministry which I sincerely hope you will think about and make your own.... First, there is the great and urgent task to hand on to the next generation the truths of our Catholic faith revealed to us by Our Lord as taught to us by the Church down the ages.

Now Cardinal Hume was a monk at Ampleforth where I was learned the Faith as a child. Nothing that I was taught was refuted by Vatican II: equally, nothing that I was taught is recognisable in the modules of *Weaving the Web*. Yet *Weaving the Web* has the *Nihil Obstat* of Monsignor Ralph Brown, Vicar General of the Diocese of Westminster; and the *imprimatur* of Monsignor Vincent Nichols, Secretary to the Conference of Bishops of England and Wales.

Neither an *imprimatur* nor a *nihil obstat* imply that those who give them agree with what is written; but they are there to assure the reader that it is free from the kind of error which might threaten the flock. It therefore enables *Weaving the Web* to be used in the Catholic schools. But just as there can be sins of ommission, so there can be error by ommission: simply from the standpoint of intellectual coherence, it is difficult to understand how Cardinal Hume can see in the Christianity described in *Weaving the Web* the 'truths of our Catholic faith ... taught to us by the Church down the ages'. Nor, if the words are to have any meaning, can *Weaving the Web* be said to be free of syncretism and indifferentism condemned by the Council, or 'that false irenicism which harms the purity of Catholic doctrine'.

'It is a miserable time,' wrote Cardinal Newman, 'when a man's Catholic profession is no voucher for his orthodoxy, and when a teacher of religion may be within the Church's pale yet external to her faith. Such has been for a season the trial of her children at various eras of history ...'[83] Such, in my view, is the trial of the English church today. Tormented by the tawdriness of its spiritual condition, and baffled by the paradoxes and mysteries of life, a generation hungers for the bread of truth. It is fed stones.

Piers Paul Read is the author of eleven novels and two works of non-fiction. He lives in London with his wife and four children. He was educated at Ampleforth College in Yorkshire and at Cambridge where he read history.

  He has served as a governor of the Cardinal Manning Boys School in North Kensington.

Notes

1. *30 Days*, January 1991.

2. John Paul II: *Redemptoris Missio*. The Mission of Christ the Redeemer.

3. *Modern Catholicism*, edited by Adrian Hastings. SPCK, London and Oxford University Press, New York. 1990, p. 132.

4. *Redemptoris Missio*. The Tablet, 2 February 1991, p.149.

5. *The Independent*, 26 January 1991. The Italics are mine.

6. *Redemptoris Missio*, op.cit.

7. Vatican II, *Sacrosanctum Concilium*, 2. From *Vatican Council II. The Conciliar and Post Conciliar Documents*. General Editor, Austin Flannery, O.P. Dominican Publications, St. Saviour's Dublin.

8. Nietszche, in *Twilight of the Gods*.

9. Vatican II, *Lumen Gentium*, 18.

10. Quoted by Anthony Rhodes in *The Vatican in the Age of the Dictators, 1922-45*. Holt, Rinehart and Winston, New York, p.339.

11. Hugh Thomas: The Spanish Civil War. Penguin Books, p.229.

12. Edward Norman in *Modern Catholicism*, p.459.

13. Sacrosanctum Concilium, 10.

14. Ibid, 47.

15. Lumen Gentium, 12.

16. Lumen Gentium, 18.

17. Lumen Gentium, 25.

18. Karl Adam: *The Spirit of Catholicism*. Translated by Dom Justin McCann, OSB. Sheed and Ward, 1929.

19. Dignitatis humanae, 1.

20. Unitatis redintegratio, 3.

21. Unitatis redintegratio, 3.

22. Augustin, Cardinal Bea: *The Unity of Christians*. Geoffrey Chapman, p.55. The italics are his.

23. Unitatis redintegratio, 24.

24. Gaudium et spes, 30.

25.   Gaudium et spes, 37.

26.   *Introduction to a Devout Life*, p.137.

27.   Gaudium et spes, 86

28.   Gaudium et spes, 68.

29.   Gaudium et spes, 68.

30.   Gaudium et spes, 71.

31.   Gaudium et spes, 39.

32.   Gaudium et spes, 42.

33.   Gaudium et spes, 25.

34.   Gaudium et spes, 86.

35.   See *Modern Catholicism*, p.248.

36.   Quoted   in   *Modern Catholicism*, p.284.

37.   For a dramatic account of his relations with the Jesuits, see *The Jesuits* by Malachi Martin.

38.   Gaudium et spes, 47.

39.   See Uta Ranke-Keinemann: Eunuchs for Heaven.   Andre Deutsche, 1990.

40.   St Francis of Sales, Op.Cit., p.160.

41.   Gustave Thibon: *What God has Joined Together*. Translated by A. Gordon Smith. Hollis and Carter, 1952, p.99.

42.   Simone de Beauvoir: *The Second Sex*. Translated and Edited by H.M. Parshley. Jonathan Cape, 1953, p.43.

43.   Matthew, V: 27-29.

44.   Gaudium et spes, 47.

45.   Laurence Stone: *Road to Divorce*. Oxford University Press, p.413.

46.   Ibid, p.415.

47.   Leo XIII,. Arcanum.

48.   Casti Connubii, 74-75.

49.   Gaudium et spes, 52.

50.   Gaudium et spes, 52.

51.   Ronald Knox: *Enthusiasm*. Oxford University Press. 1950, p.20.

52.   Women and the Priesthood, Vatican City, 1976, p.13.

53.   Corinthians 11: 7-9.

54.   Ephesians, 5: 21-22.

55.   1 Timothy: 2: 14.

56.   1 Peter: 3:1.

57.   1 Peter, 3:6.

58.   Dei Verbum, 11.

59. E. Schillebeeckx: Marriage: Secular Reality and Saving Mystery. Sheed and Ward, 1965, p.271.

60. Matthew, 19:4-6.

61. Ivan Illich: *Gender*, Marion Boyars, 1983, p.16.

62. A.C. Robin Skynner, M.B., F.R.C.Psych., D.P.M. One Flesh: Separate Persons. Principles of Family and Marital Psycholtherapy. Constable, 1976.

63. John McDade, S.J. in *Moderen Catholicism*, op.cit., p. 423.

64. Lord Macaulay: *Critical and Historical Essays.* Collins, 1965, p.275.

65. Thomas a Kempis: *The Imitation of Christ*. Penguin Books.

66. .Luke, 10: 21.

67. Among them should be included Segundo, Sobrino, Gutierriez, Boff, together with sympathisers like Schillebeeckx and Kung.

68. Sacrosanctum Concilium, 2.

69. Matthew, 25:41-43.

70. Weaving the Web, Teacher's Book, p.11.

71. Weaving the Web, Community, Story, People, Level 1, p.71.

72. Teacher's Book, p.52.

73. Presbytororum Ordinis, 2.

74. Community, Story, People, Level 3, p.19.

75. Lumen Gentium, 8.

76. Community, Story, People, Level 3, p.26.

77. Communication, Celebration, Values, Level 2, p.31.

78. Community, Story, People, Level 2, p.14.

79. Community, Story, People, Level 2, p.8.

80. Communications, Celebration, Values, Level 3, p.62-63.

81. Community, Story, People, Level 2, p.18

82. Lumen Gentium, 28.

83. *A Form of Infidelity of the Day*.